The Cat Dictionary

The Cat Dictionary

Peter Mandel

illustrated by Annette Busse

PENGUIN BOOKS

PENGUIN BOOKS

Published by the Penguin Group
Penguin Books Ltd, 27 Wrights Lane, London W8 5TZ, England
Penguin Books USA Inc., 375 Hudson Street, New York, New York 10014, USA
Penguin Books Australia Ltd, Ringwood, Victoria, Australia
Penguin Books Canada Ltd, 10 Alcorn Avenue, Toronto, Ontario, Canada M4V 3B2
Penguin Books (NZ) Ltd, 182-190 Wairau Road, Auckland 10, New Zealand
Penguin Books, Amethyst Street, Theta Ext 1, Johannesburg, South Africa

Penguin Books Ltd, Registered Offices: Harmondsworth, Middlesex, England

First published by Penguin Books 1994

ISBN 0 140 24661 4

Electronic origination by Iskova Image Setting
Printed and bound by Creda Press

For Geoffrey and Jenny

Acknowledgements

This book would not have been possible without the many excellent ideas supplied by my agent, Emmy Jacobson, who was tinkering with a cat dictionary concept at about the same time I began toying with it.

Some of the definitions included in the book appeared in *CATS Magazine*, in a slightly different form, under the heading, 'Sharpen Up Your Cat Vocabulary'.

Introduction

The Cat Dictionary owes its existence to the fact that the mind tends to wander when one is forced to page through a yellowing *Webster's* or a barbell-sized *Oxford English Dictionary* in search of 'definitions'. And when one is a bad speller like I am, the simplest word search can drag on as you try to zero in on the correct letters involved.

Then, all of a sudden, you find yourself among cats of all kinds — catamounts, catcalls, catamarans — and you imagine a book you'd much rather be reading than the one you have in hand. Perhaps one with nice, bold pictures of Siamese sunning themselves or Manx leaping onto couches in place of those minuscule line drawings that say things like *Figure 2* beneath them. Maybe a volume that doesn't waste page after page on dogs, fish, geraniums and hot-air balloons. And, most important, one where each and every entry begins with **C-A-T**, so there's no need for wild guessing about spelling.

I hope that, for you, **The Cat Dictionary** fulfils these all-important requirements.

catatonic

What your feline drinks on the rocks with gin: It's made, not surprisingly, from the *catawba*, a light red Mediterranean grape.

caterpillar

That eyesore you bought at the pet shop which is covered in orange carpeting and which your cat is supposed to use as a scratching post. In fact, your feline prefers to use furniture for this purpose.

*cat*astrophe

A prize given annually to the cat that engineers the most spectacular domestic disaster. Last year, the honour went to Muffin of Cape Town for knocking a priceless Ming vase off the mantel, denting the hand-laid parquet floor, and tripping the burglar alarm an hour before dawn.

*cat*tail

The feline version of a 'fish story'. It's told, most often, by a sympathetic family member attempting to cover up your pet's role in a ***cat*astrophe**.

catarrh

The menacing sound made by your feline on encountering another cat strolling arrogantly across your front lawn.

category

A word used to describe your bruised and bloodied pet after it loses a fight against that same cat that was strolling arrogantly across your front lawn.

CAT scan

What your feline does immediately upon entering the kitchen or dining room. In two or three seconds, the average *CAT* scan will disclose every morsel of food available and compute the quickest route to obtaining it.

catapult

Any piece of furniture that your pet tends to use as a springboard while tearing around the house like a maniac. Popular choices include the backs of antique wing chairs and sofa cushions.

CAT scan

*cat*aract

The Academy Award-winning performance your cat puts on about an hour before any regularly scheduled feeding. It usually includes a barrage of overly dramatic ***cat*erwauls**.

*cat*acomb

The disgusting, hair-clotted instrument you use to groom your feline — that is, if you don't mind getting violently scratched.

cat-o'-nine-tails

Any feline that is unable to walk across a coffee table or kitchen counter without knocking everything off.

*cat*sup

What you mumble to yourself, between yawns, when you hear ear-rings and perfume bottles falling off the bureau at 5.00 am.

*cat*alepsy

A medical condition common in indoor cats and characterized by sudden bizarre seizures and bursts of energy. It is most often observed shortly after mealtime.

*cat*alogue

What your cat leaves behind when it vacates the litter box.

catalepsy

*cata*clysm

A devastating flood caused by an attempt to shampoo your pet in either the bath-tub or bathroom sink. Usually, water is distributed throughout the house as your cat flees to its favourite hiding place.

*cat*walk

Your feline's habitual route that traverses the top of your neighbour's fence, goes along your neighbour's driveway and into your neighbour's basement through an open window.

*cat*call

Your neighbour informing you of your pet's most recent **catwalk**.

*cat*bird seat

Your feline's favourite chair for observing sparrows feasting at your backyard feeder.

*cat*kin

Any species of animal that has whiskers, a tail and that takes pride in napping at least 18 hours a day.

catbird seat

*cat*amount

The total amount of household furnishings shredded by your cat's incessant claw sharpening.

*cat*ty-corner

The area in your kitchen which has been completely taken over by your feline's litter box and the pungent odours which emanate from it.

*cat*nip

A feline's not-so-friendly way of informing you that you had better stop scratching its fluffy white tummy, or else.

*cat*fish

The grilled salmon fillet you placed on the counter momentarily that, seconds later, was mysteriously missing a large, jagged chunk.

*cat*ty

The stray cat that follows you throughout the back nine on your local golf course. Its speciality seems to be pouncing on unusually promising putts.

*Cat*skills

The full range of your pet's mouse-chasing, bird-pouncing (and snack-begging) abilities.

cat burglar

A thieving feline fond of absconding with morsels of Swiss cheese and stuffed olives from an unattended hors-d'oeuvre tray.

*cat*abolism

The sum of your pet's bodily processes (and the reason it requires an infusion of calories every half hour).

cat burglar

*cat*tle

That noisy, plastic cat toy which your feline completely ignores except for the brief period when you are just on the verge of dropping off to sleep.

*cat*achreses

Unsightly folds or wrinkles at the bottom of a bedspread that used to be quite crisp before your cat began sacking out there on a nightly basis.

*cat*alpa

Any family member that can be counted on to allow an occasional sliver of roast chicken to slip from his fingertips to the floor.

*cat*ch-all

A nickname given to felines who specialize in retrieving those slivers of roast chicken.

*cat*alase

The shoe-string of your left sneaker that's frayed beyond recognition due to your pet's obsessive clawing and nibbling.

*cat*harsis

A process whereby cat hair is purged from navy blue wool clothing by frantic brushing, cursing and hopping up and down.

cat's cradle

Another name for your laundry basket when it's half-full of warm bath towels fresh from the drier.

*cat*alytic converter

One of those aerosol products designed to neutralize odour when sprayed on stains left by your pet. You can tell it's working by the presence of the sickly sweet cover-up scent.

*cat*gut

The sagging, basketball-sized digestive organ common in domestic felines.

*cat*tleya

What your pet will do, through half-closed lids, should you cross the room carrying an overstuffed tuna sandwich.

cat rig

That new pet door you installed to allow your cat to come and go as it pleases, but which has the added benefit of allowing every stray in the neighbourhood to stop by at their convenience.

*cat*amenial

A term for chores such as emptying the litter box, vacuuming up fur balls, and hauling 10 kg bags of dry food home from the supermarket.

at rig

catering

The highly dangerous habit of feeding your pet on demand rather than at anything remotely resembling mealtime.

Catalina

Any feline that, while settling on your lap, has the obnoxious habit of resting its full weight against one or the other of your upper thighs.

cool *cat*

A phrase describing the demeanour of the domestic feline when confronted with children, small dogs or a dish of generic dry food.

lap *cat*

The pet you had as a child which insisted on running in circles around your living room, and which eventually made a highly decorative pathway in the nap of your mother's wall-to-wall carpeting.

*cat*brier

That sparse, rather sick-looking plant you've been trying to cultivate but which your pet has singled out for relentless leaf-chewing and root excavation.

*cat*aplasm

The shapeless mass of semi-organic material that your cat coughs up along with a nice, juicy fur ball.

alley *cat*

The resident pet down at Joe's Bowling World and Bar & Grill.

cat got your tongue

A likely explanation for the disappearance of several slices from a package of delicatessen meat.

*cat*talo

A form of greeting, common to the domesticated feline, consisting of a plaintive whine followed by brisk rubbing of the teeth and gums against the corner of a coffee table.

*cat*enary

A mythical beast combining the head of a cat with the body of a canary. According to Greek legend, it perished after trying to swallow its tail.

*cat*boat

What your feline envisions as it gingerly prods a bone-china teacup floating in a sink full of dirty dishes.

*cat*echu

A feline sneeze (often the result of excessive ***cat*mint** inhalation).

*Cat*holic

Any feline that indulges in a fish dinner each and every Friday.

*cat*aplexy

A sudden seizure often experienced by indoor cats. It's normally characterized by moans, yowls, Olympic-sized leaps, and frenetic scrambling across tile floors and up staircases.

catechist

The rough, sandpapery lick your pet bestows on you after you've fed it a generous helping of smoked trout.

catamaran

A pejorative term for a feline who has taken The Official Cat I.Q. Test and come out with an I.Q. score of 15 or below.

copy-*cat*

Any feline that, at the first sign of afternoon nap activity, yawns and stretches out on the particular couch in use (taking up prime pillow space or valuable foot room).

*cat*ching

The erratic kicking activity your feline engages in with its back leg when attempting to scratch an itch located somewhere between its shoulderblades and rear end.

*cat*box

An empty carton, *any* carton, containing a sheet or two of crinkly tissue paper and some snippets of ribbon.

*cat*house

Same as ***cat*box**, except the carton is turned on its side and ends up becoming a fixture in your front hallway as your pet's preferred hideaway.

fat *cat*

A phrase describing a primarily sedentary feline that consumes at least four bowls of canned food daily. Some scientists estimate that between 92% and 98% of indoor cats could be said to fall into this **category.**

at *cat*

*cat*alyst

Any collection of vocabulary words that makes a big deal of the simple fact that each has the word *cat* in it.